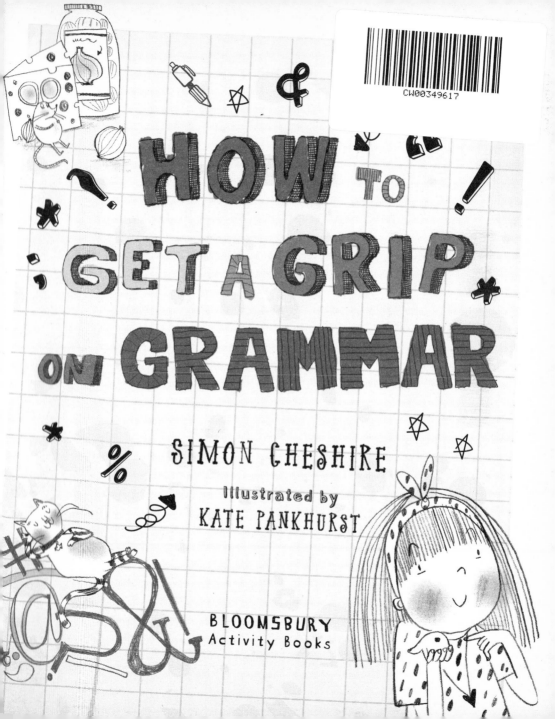

HOW TO GET A GRIP ON GRAMMAR

SIMON CHESHIRE

Illustrated by
KATE PANKHURST

BLOOMSBURY
Activity Books

Published 2015 by Bloomsbury Publishing Plc

50 Bedford Square, London, WC1B 3DP

www.bloomsbury.com

Bloomsbury is a registered trademark of Bloomsbury Publishing Plc

ISBN 978-1-4088-6255-1

A CIP record for this book is available from the British Library.

MIX

Paper from
responsible sources

FSC® C020471

Printed and bound in Great Britain by CPI Group (UK) Ltd, Croydon CR0 4YY

1 3 5 7 9 10 8 6 4 2

CONTENTS

INTRODUCTION

Welcome to the world of grammar!

This book is designed to help you understand the **basics** of English grammar. We'll be looking at four topics:

✴ **Words:** The building blocks of language

✴ **Punctuation:** Symbols that help us organise those words

✴ **Sentences:** The structure that helps us create communication

✴ Other useful grammatical bits and pieces

Throughout this book are loads of ideas and activities to help you get to grips with grammar.

So what are you waiting for – let's get started!

CHAPTER 1
WHY DO WE NEED GRAMMAR?

Your mission:
to polish up your writing and put a shine on your sentences!

Terrific toolkit

Grammar is a very important part of language. It's all very well having an endless list of words, but we need to put them together in a way that makes sense.

If we didn't use grammar, all we'd be able to do is point at things and say, "tree", or "friend." Grammar is a toolkit, which helps us put words together to create meaningful communication.

Before we dive into the world of grammar, we need to remember one thing:

⭐ Grammar isn't a totally fixed set of rules. ⭐

Grammar helps **standardise** a language, to regulate and oversee it, so that everyone using the language knows **how** to use it. But grammar **changes** over time.

It adapts to new words and new ways of expressing ourselves. English is a living, evolving, exciting, vivid language. In everyday life, nobody speaks and writes with *perfect* grammar *all* the time. We should all aim to be grammatically correct, in speech and on paper, because good grammar is vital for keeping our communication **clear**.

However, grammar isn't always about having unbreakable laws that are set in stone forever, otherwise we'd all still be talking like the Tudors!

CHAPTER 2
WORDS

Words used in English generally fall into one of **eight** categories, or **parts of speech**. These are the basic building blocks of the English language. Some people divide words into nine or even ten categories, but the following eight are used the most:

➊ Nouns

A noun is a word which refers to a *thing*. (Usually a person, place or object, and sometimes an event.)

For example:

✬ *Dave, Charlotte, John, Chloe, Fred, London, Barcelona, China.*

These are all **proper nouns** (sometimes called 'proper names') and are nouns which indicate a specific person or place. They always begin with a capital letter.

✦ *House, shovel, plate, spaceship, statue, pen, horse, book.*

These are all nouns because they refer to objects.

✦ *Flood, discovery, invasion.*

These are nouns that refer to things which are events. This sort of noun can be tricky to identify, because they have 'matching' verbs.

For example: "My discovery amazed everyone."

Discovery is a noun here, because it refers to a **thing** (the thing that you discovered).

"I discovered an ancient temple."

However, in this sentence, *discovered* is a verb, because it's something you **did**.

Nouns can be either **singular** or **plural**:

Singular means that the noun is talking about **one** thing: *dog, fence, shed, pen, stick.*

Plural means that the noun is talking about more than one thing: *dogs, fences, sheds, pens, sticks.*

11

ACTIVITY

Open a book at random and see if you can pick out every noun on the page. Use the space provided to make your list.

_____ _____ _____

_____ _____ _____

_____ _____ _____

_____ _____ _____

_____ _____ _____

_____ _____ _____

_____ _____ _____

_____ _____ _____

_____ _____ _____

_____ _____ _____

_____ _____ _____

_____ _____ _____

 Make a list of nouns which have 'matching' verbs.

Can you come up with some sentences to show the difference between the two?

For example:

Noun: The *invasion* of Earth happened at dinnertime.

Verb: The aliens *invaded* Earth while we were having dinner.

NOUNS   ### VERBS

_____   _____

_____   _____

_____   _____

_____   _____

_____   _____

_____   _____

_____   _____

_____   _____

_____   _____

_____   _____

_____   _____

ACTIVITY

Come up with as many nouns as you can that are associated with these topics. Time yourself and see how many you can get for each topic in just one minute!

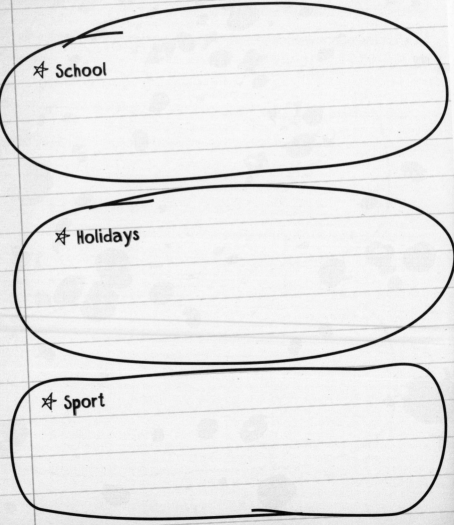

☆ School

☆ Holidays

☆ Sport

✿ Animals

✿ Your bedroom

✿ Food

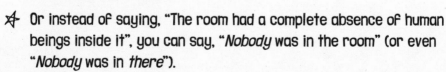

② Pronouns

A pronoun is a word which takes the place of a noun, or which is a substitute for having to use lots of nouns together.

(I, me, my, you, they, it, something, there, nobody, them, yourself, that, who, none, which – all of these are pronouns, because all of them can be used in place of a noun or multiple nouns.)

For example:

⚝ Instead of saying, "Ken, Mary, Mohammed, Josh and Katie ate ice creams", you can use a pronoun in place of all those names and say, "*They* ate ice creams".

⚝ Or instead of saying, "The room had a complete absence of human beings inside it", you can say, "*Nobody* was in the room" (or even "*Nobody* was in *there*").

Change the following sentences to use pronouns instead of nouns where possible.

Beware! If you change *all* the nouns, you might find the sentence doesn't make sense any more.

 Arthur, Jane and Sophie stood in the field while the goats ran around each person.

_____

 When the person writing this sentence has finished, that person will go for a walk.

_____

 Every story liked by Catherine was really scary.

_____

 David played video games with Paul, then David and Paul had beans on toast.

_____

 Three of the workmen finished building the wall while one of their fellow workmen made cups of tea.

_____

_____

6 "We don't like Maths, Science, English or History," said Lenny and Mike.

7 Most of this class agree with Miss Smith and Mr Johnson that reading a good book is much better than watching telly.

8 Where does that very tall girl live?

9 When Jim looked into the box, Jim discovered that all the fleas had escaped.

10 If George eats any more mashed potato there won't be any mashed potato left for Carrie or Elaine.

(Pssst! Notice how the order of words sometimes needs to change.)

Pronouns are very useful, because:

1 They make it possible to talk about **yourself** and **others** without sounding a bit **silly**.

For example, if your name is Harry you don't need to say, "Harry needs to sneeze". Instead you can say, "*I* need to sneeze".

Or, instead of saying to Isobel, "Does Isobel like pizza?" you can say "Do *you* like pizza?"

2 They make it possible to talk about things that are **unknown,** **forgotten** or **undecided**.

For example, you can say, "We've got to think of *something* – fast!"

Instead of, "We've got to think of a possible scheme, plan of action, or effective strategy – fast!"

Or, "*These* are too big, have you got *anything* smaller?"

Instead of saying, "The shoes placed in William's hands are excessive in size, does sales assistant have shoes of smaller dimensions?"

19

ACTIVITY

Pick out the pronouns in the following sentences. Make a list of the pronouns you find in the space provided.

1 You know, that reminds me of something he said to his mum.

2 They were all there – nobody can claim they didn't see the aliens land in her swimming pool.

3 It doesn't matter whether it's you, me or that lazy friend of yours who takes the dog for a walk.

4 I was very upset because nobody came to my party.

5 Didn't you get top marks in the test?

6 Daisy thought that nobody was looking, so she took two slices of cake and ate both of them.

7 When the dinner ladies asked me about the gravy, I told them it was delicious.

8 His friend has a pet rabbit who performs magic tricks.

9 Their house was full of his clothes, her computers, and the souvenirs they had collected during their holidays.

10 You may find it funny, Jane, but nobody is laughing.

PRONOUNS

_____ _____ _____
_____ _____ _____
_____ _____ _____
_____ _____ _____
_____ _____ _____
_____ _____ _____
_____ _____ _____
_____ _____ _____
_____ _____ _____
_____ _____ _____
_____ _____ _____
_____ _____ _____
_____ _____ _____
_____ _____ _____
_____ _____ _____

ACTIVITY

Use the space provided to try writing some sentences which don't include any pronouns at all.

(It's much harder than you might think!)

✩ "Steve can't play football today."

✩ "Mum always enjoys fixing the car."

✩ "Mr Smith patiently waited for the doors to open."

It's possible to sub-divide pronouns into several separate types:

Personal pronouns: Words which refer to people.

For example, *me, you, myself, us, we, I, him, her, they*.

Possessive pronouns: Words which refer to what people have, or possess.

For example, *their, our, mine, yours, his, hers*.

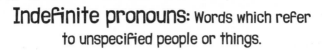

Indefinite pronouns: Words which refer to unspecified people or things.

For example, *something, nothing, everybody, many, both, more, most.*

There are *lots* of other types as well! The thing you need to remember is that all pronouns, no matter what type they are, are **'noun-substitutes'** - they stand in for a noun or a group of nouns.

③ Verbs

A verb is a word which tells us about an action, or about a 'state of being' (how something is).

For example:

★ *Run, jump, drive, talk, sit, wobble, taste, explore, tumble, press, kick, shake.*

These are all verbs which indicate an **action**, or something **happening**.

★ *Is, am, are, was, were, be, being, been, have.*

These are verbs which denote how something is, its 'state of being'.

There are only a few of these **'state of being'** verbs. In fact, the first eight are all really just variations of the one verb: **'IS'** - you'll see why in this next bit.

26

Verbs change according to the **tense**. In other words, they change depending on whether the action (or 'state') they describe is happening now, or at another time.

Present tense (happening now): *He burps, I am, they skip, she writes, we are, he laughs.*

Past tense (happened some time ago): *He burped, I was, they skipped, she wrote, we were, he laughed.*

Future tense (will happen at some point): *He will burp, I will be, they will skip, she will write, we will be, he will laugh.*

Most of those 'state of being' verbs are the same verb: '*To be*'

They are expressed in different tenses and by different speakers:

Present tense: *I am, he is, we are.*
Past tense: *I was, he was, we were.*
Future tense: *I will be, he will be, we will be.*

27

1. I'm walking to the shops and buying the latest issue of my favourite magazine.

2. Fred is one of those people who always makes a mess in the kitchen.

3. I like Amy, and I like Annabel, but my best friend is definitely Lucy.

4. I'm sure my dad is getting me a games console for my birthday.

5. There are lots of sports played in the park on Sundays.

6. The recycling lorry comes on a Friday, so we put out our waste paper the night before.

7. I really enjoy doing activities that help me improve my grammar.

8. Jake takes a long time to comb his hair.

9. I see my friend on the way to school and I run to catch up with him.

10. Tina cycles to school but Nancy takes the bus.

WORDS

PAST TENSE

1. _____

2. _____

3. _____

4. _____

5. _____

6. _____

7. _____

8. _____

9. _____

10. _____

FUTURE TENSE

1. _____
_____
2. _____
_____
3. _____
_____
4. _____
_____
5. _____
_____
6. _____
_____
7. _____
_____
8. _____
_____
9. _____
_____
10. _____
_____

Verbs can also change according to voice.
They can be **active** or **passive**.

For example:

✩ "Mrs Jenkins teaches Zog the robot".

Mrs Jenkins is the one who is doing something
(teaching) and the verb 'teaches' is active.

BUT...

✩ "Zog the robot is taught by Mrs Jenkins".

Mrs Jenkins is still the one doing something
(she's still teaching),
but here the
verb is *passive*.

Verbs can change
depending on how you
need to express them.

31

Use the space provided to rewrite these sentences by changing the verbs from **active** to **passive**:

  The police officer chases the bank robber.

② The pilot flies the aeroplane through the clouds.

③ The fastest runner wins the race.

④ The Prime Minister speaks to parliament.

32

(5) The bear growls at the tortoise.

(6) The cinema is showing a movie.

(7) The hungry cat follows the little mouse.

(8) Dad cooks my dinner.

(9) Peter writes on the paper.

(10) While playing football, Joanne tackles Matt.

Below is a jumble of nouns. Pick out two at a time, and join them together by using a suitable verb.

For example: Mum **drives** the car, or John **uses** his phone.

fish · Dad · book · brother
desk · kettle · hurricane · car
phone · swamp · teacher
duck · squirrel
John · notepad · friend
Jennifer · scissors
pencil · toffee · paper
Chris · shirt · radio · computer · shop
garden · house
carrot · monster
boat · box
Mum · Nicola
postman · explosion · sister · auntie

34

 Open a book at random and see if you can pick out every verb on the page. Use the space provided to make your list.

Adjectives and Adverbs

Adjectives and adverbs are words which *describe* things.

❹ Adjectives

An adjective is a word which adds description to a noun.

They can describe . . .

⭐ Size and shape: *Big, small, tall, short, narrow, tiny, enormous, round, flat.*

⭐ Age and origin: *Old, new, young, ancient, French, Martian.*

⭐ Colours and numbers: *Blue, red, green, one, two, three.*

⭐ Materials: *Woollen, atomic, nuclear, metallic.*

⭐ Physical properties: *Rough, smooth, scratchy, loud, ugly, beautiful, wet.*

⭐ Non-physical properties: *Perfect, interesting, cheap, expensive, wealthy, sad, happy.*

And many other qualities or attributes which a person or object might have.

"I live in a garden shed." If you add adjectives to this you get, "I live in a *little, grey, wooden* garden shed."

"I saw a movie at a cinema with my friend." If you add adjectives to this you get, "I saw a *funny* movie at a *big* cinema with my *talkative* friend."

ACTIVITY

Below is a list of nouns. Add as many descriptive adjectives to them as you can – even a few wacky ones!

For example: To the noun 'goat' you could add adjectives such as *clever, hairy, dangerous, robotic* . . .

Light bulb ....

Pond ....

Painting ....

Mug ....

Jacket ....

Man ....

Tree ....

Lizard ....

Superhero ....

Face ....

There's a special type of adjective called an **article**, sometimes called a **determiner**. There are three of them, and they go in front of nouns.

In English, we use two **indefinite articles**:

'**A**' and '**An**' (*a* cat, *an* apple etc.)

We use one **definite article**:

'**The**' (*the* sky, *the* river, *the* alien etc.)

❺ Adverbs

An adverb is a word which adds description to a *verb*, in the same way as an adjective adds description to a *noun*.

Like adjectives, there are a huge variety of adverbs. Examples of adverbs added to **verbs** might be:

✦ My teacher speaks [verb] *quietly* [adverb] (or *softly, gently, harshly, sharply*).

✦ We *quickly* [adverb] swam [verb] away from the shark (or *rapidly, hurriedly, frantically*).

✦ I play [verb] the piano *beautifully* [adverb] (or *elegantly, delightfully, badly, terribly*).

Rewrite the following sentences so that they include one or two adverbs. The verbs have been underlined for you.

For example: "He <u>walked</u> to school", could become, "He <u>walked</u> *slowly* and *carefully* to school".

① My friend <u>bakes</u> cakes.

_____

② I have a pet monkey who <u>speaks</u> English.

_____

③ Auntie Val runs for miles, then <u>drinks</u> water.

_____

④ William <u>reads</u> the words on the page.

_____

⑤ I <u>write</u> my emails before <u>phoning</u> my friend.

_____

_____

6 Callum <u>sinks</u> into the swamp.

7 Nellie <u>walks</u> out onto the stage to <u>dance</u> and <u>sing</u>.

8 Mum <u>drives</u> the car into town.

9 The cat <u>sleeps</u> in the shade.

10 Shirley <u>plays</u> chess.

Some (not all) adjectives and adverbs can be used to make **comparisons**; to show how the nouns or verbs they are applied to can be compared to others.

For example:

✪ Big (adjective): "This is a *big* elephant", could also describe how big something is, compared to others: "This is a *bigger* elephant than the other one", or, "This is the *biggest* elephant in the world".

Another example, "It's a *warm* day", could become, "It's a *warmer* day than yesterday", or, "It's the *warmest* day since records began".

43

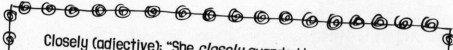

Closely (adjective): "She *closely* guarded her secret", could also describe *how* well guarded that secret was compared to others: "She guarded her secret *more closely* than her jewels", or, "She kept the *most closely* guarded secret on Earth".

Another example, "The lion roared *angrily*", could become, "The lion roared *more angrily* than the cat", or, "That's the *most angrily* roaring lion I've ever heard".

These comparisons can work the opposite way too: "He's a *popular* teacher", can become, "He's a *less popular* teacher than Mrs Smith", or, "He's the *least popular* teacher we've ever had at this school".

□   **WORDS**

 Rewrite each of the following sentences using the comparative forms of the adjective or adverb.

1. That was a *silly* dance!

_____

_____

2. I heard an *interesting* discussion the other day.

_____

_____

3. It was a *slow* journey from our house to the seaside.

_____

_____

4. I bought a *large* bar of chocolate from the corner shop.

_____

_____

★

5. My uncle is a *polite* man.

_____

_____

6. Ultra-Battle-Toad is an *evil* super villain.

_____

_____

7. This is a *beautiful* painting.

_____

_____

8. I saw a *long* snake at the zoo.

_____

_____

9. I want a TV with a *wide* screen.

_____

_____

10. Visiting the museum was a *strange* experience.

_____

_____

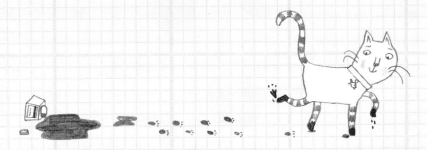

This ability to compare doesn't apply to *all* adjectives and adverbs. For example, you can't make comparisons using the following:

Iron: "Her iron sword shone in her hand."

You can't say, "Her sword was more iron-ish . . ."

Totally: "I totally ruined my trousers."

It doesn't make sense to say, "I've more totally ruined . . ."

Electronic: "He brought his electronic calculator to school."

You couldn't have, "His most electronic calculator"
They all work using electricity!

Dead: "The dead body was found in the library."

Having a, "dead-est body" or a, "least dead body" isn't possible!

⑥ Prepositions

A preposition is a linking word. It links a noun (or a pronoun) to other words by showing how the noun is *related* to something else. In other words, prepositions show how a noun is linked to whatever else is going on in the rest of the sentence. (Examples of prepositions are *above, in, at, to, near, by, after, from, with, below, up, until, for, beside, against, during, inside.*)

For example:

✣ "The class walked **to** school **on** Friday."

'**To**' shows the link between the class and where they walked.

'**On**' shows the link between their walk to school and when it happened.

✣ "I was **near** the shop when the cow ran **inside** to buy some milk."

'**Near**' shows how I'm linked to the shop.

'**Inside**' shows how the cow is linked to it.

The *links, or relationships,* that prepositions show often fall into two types:

1. They link up nouns or pronouns to **where** things are. (She was *in* the garden)

2. They link up nouns or pronouns to **when** things happen. (She was in the garden *after* dinner)

 ACTIVITY

Insert prepositions into the blank spaces below. If you find it easier use the space provided to rewrite the sentences with all of the correct prepositions in place.

1. Lionel was waiting _____ the bus _____ school.

2. I cycled _____ London _____ Birmingham. I set off _____ nine o'clock.

3. Mum was born _____ the year 1990. In this photo, she is _____ my grandmother.

4. _____ lunch we drove _____ the beach.

5. We won't be going _____ the school trip _____ the stolen money is returned.

6. Steve stood _____ Evan, who was sitting _____ the table.

7. They took their seats _____ the spaceship and it flew _____ Earth _____ the Moon.

8. John fetched a blanket _____ the cupboard and placed it _____ the bed.

9. Bill argued _____ Richard _____ their holiday.

10. His work in Rocket Science was _____ the average _____ the class.

1. _____

2. _____

3. _____

4. _____

5. _____

6. _____

7. _____

8. _____

9. _____

10. _____

Are there any different prepositions you could have used instead? This is tricky! Use the space provided to rewrite the sentences, this time using *different* prepositions to the ones you used before.

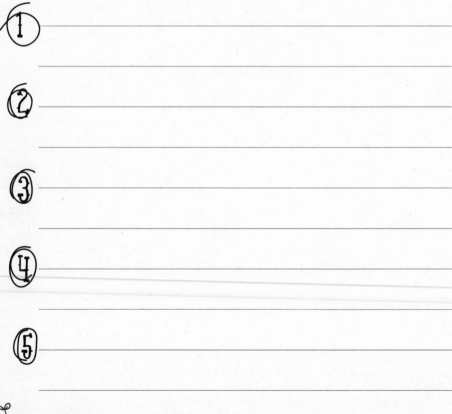

WORDS

6 _____

7 _____

8 _____

9 _____

⭐

10 _____

 ⭐

53

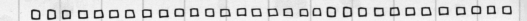

⑦ Conjunctions

A conjunction is a word which links whole sentences or clauses together (turn to page 112 to find out more on clauses). Both prepositions and conjunctions are linking words, but conjunctions are different to prepositions because conjunctions 'clip together' *whole groups* of words, whereas prepositions link up one specific object or idea. (*And, but, although, if, so, or, either, unless, both, because,* are all examples of conjunctions.)

for example:

✴ Instead of saying, "He was an intelligent boy. He got every answer wrong", we can use a conjunction to join the two ideas and say, "He was an intelligent boy **but** he got every answer wrong" (or "... **although** he got every answer wrong").

✴ Instead of, "You can have peas with custard. You can use the toilet later", you could say, "You can have peas with custard **and** you can use the toilet later" (or "... **so** you can use the toilet later").

ACTIVITY

Rewrite the following sentences in the space provided so that they include conjunctions to join the sentences together.

1. Mrs Jones is our teacher. We had a lesson on grammar.

2. A mole dug up our lawn. It didn't dig up our neighbour's lawn.

3. There's a monster behind you. I think you should run.

4. I drink a glass of milk every day. I never drink a glass of vinegar.

5. He doesn't like animals. He looks after his neighbour's gerbil.

6. Sam got up late. It was Tuesday.

7. The bus drove past. Fred was waiting at the bus stop.

8. The thief ran away. The detective chased the thief.

9. I did not laugh. My brother was covered in mud.

10. Can you see her? Has she gone?

WORDS

1. _____

2. _____

3. _____

4. _____

5. _____

6. _____

7. _____

8. _____

9. _____

10. _____

Now try re-wording the sentences so that you can use different conjunctions to join them.

① _____

_____

② _____

_____

③ _____

_____

④ _____

_____

⑤ _____

_____

6

7

8

9

10

❽ Interjections

An interjection is a word which is only present to express an emotion.
(They are 'outburst' words such as, *Ouch! Ow! Hey! Oi! Hah! Aha!*)

For example:

✦ **Oi!** You there! Come back with my sandwich!

✦ **Aha!** I've found an important clue!

✦ **Ouch!** These pants are full of drawing pins!

✦ **Ow!** I knew I shouldn't have twisted my leg like that!

✦ **Hey!** You're that famous movie star, aren't you?

✦ Call that a talking frog? **Hah!** My cat talks better than that!

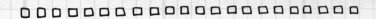

Interjections do not include words such as *zap, pow, bang, crash*. A word like this, which imitates a sound, is called an

onomatopoeia

(pronounced on-o-mat-o-pee-a).

Here's a head-scratcher!

Although it is true that words in English usually fall into the **eight** categories we've just looked at, it is also important to look at what a word **does** in a sentence and not just what the word **is**. Sometimes the **same word** can function as two (or more!) different parts of speech.

For example:

✳ **Run:** "I went for a run" – In this sentence, 'run' is a noun (a run).

"I can run fast" – However in this sentence, 'run' is a verb (I'm doing some running).

Quite a lot of words can function as both a verb and a noun:

Book: "I'm reading a book" [noun]/ "I'll book those tickets" [verb]

Set: "Ben has a set of toy cars" [noun]/ "Ben waited for the jelly to set until he ate it" [verb]

✳ **Any:** "Have you got any pants?" – In this sentence 'any' is an adjective (it says something about the noun 'pants').

"Arthur didn't buy a pizza because there wasn't any left" – However in this sentence 'any' is a pronoun (it stands in place of repeating the noun 'pizza').

✴ **All**: "All pop stars sing" – In this sentence, 'all' is an adjective (it describes the number of pop stars).

"Jake lost all he owned in the flood" – However in this sentence, 'all' is a noun (it's the total of the things he lost).

✴ The following two words are examples which have several functions:

Well:

Adverb: "My exams went well."

Interjection: "Well, well, well, what have we here?"

Noun: "Oh dear, I've fallen down a well."

Verb: "Tears well in my eyes when I taste Dad's cooking."

Down:

Preposition: "Lily lives down the street".

Adverb: "Lily fell down."

Noun: "Lily's pillow is stuffed with down."

Interjection: "Down, Spot, down!"

If you're not sure about a word's correct part of speech, the question to ask is: **what is this word doing in the sentence? What is it *here* for?**

Can you think of some words that can be more than one part of speech?

For example:

Noun: What is today's *date*?

Verb: Can you *date* this antique school dinner?

Use the space provided to write some sentences to show the difference.

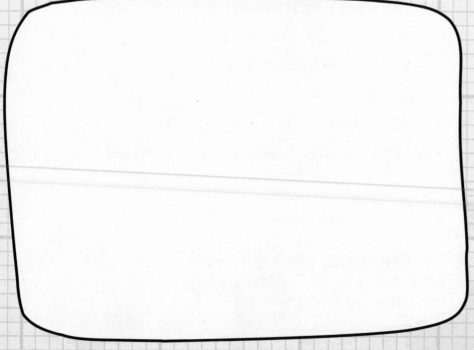

CHAPTER 3
PUNCTUATION

Now we've got a grip on words, we need to know about **punctuation** - the collection of symbols used to help us **organise, group** and **clarify** words.

Did you know?

It's thought that the world's first punctuation appeared in Ancient Chinese texts. They used a little black block as a full stop, and a symbol that looked a bit like a capital 'L' to mark the end of a chapter.

It's believed that punctuation was originally created to help people who were reading text out loud (because in those days very few people could read or write).

Full stop

A **full stop** like this, .
has only one function. It ends a
sentence. A sentence like this
one.

The first word of a sentence,
including one which follows a full
stop, should have a capital letter.

The only other time you can
use a full stop is to indicate an
abbreviation.

For example:

Prof: An abbreviation of Professor.

Sgt.: Short for Sergeant.

e.g.: Meaning 'for example' (it actually stands for *exempli
gratia* which is a phrase in Latin).

Place full stops in the text below so that it makes sense. Don't forget to include capital letters! If you find it easier, use the space provided to rewrite the text with all of the full stops in place.

Jamal and Sarah ran around the playground they kicked a ball to each other football was Jamal's favourite game he was on the school team Sarah was a good football player too she sent Jamal some very accurate shots they were both concentrating on their game so much that they didn't hear the whistle blow their teacher had to blow the whistle again

Exclamation mark

An **exclamation mark** like this, ! comes at the end
of a sentence in place of a full stop. It usually indicates emotion,
just like an interjection (see page 60) but can also indicate
something dramatic, an order, or simply something loud.

For example:

✴ The pile of glasses fell over with a deafening crash! [Noise]

✴ Suddenly, standing there in the doorway was the evil Dr. Nastiperson! [Drama]

✴ Oh, no way, man! That is well out of order! [Emotion]

✴ You there! Put that chocolate cake down! [Order]

The following sentences all have an exclamation mark at the end of them instead of a full stop. Can you decide which ones indicate noise, drama, emotion or an order?

Be careful – some of them might indicate more than one of these!

The car screeched around the corner!
noise/drama/emotion/order

You've got to be kidding!
noise/drama/emotion/order

He sank into an armchair and burst into tears!
noise/drama/emotion/order

Stop making that awful racket!
noise/drama/emotion/order

70

Begin writing your answers . . . now!
noise/drama/emotion/order

BANG!
noise/drama/emotion/order

There was no way out: they were trapped!
noise/drama/emotion/order

For the last time, leave it alone!
noise/drama/emotion/order

Forget it!
noise/drama/emotion/order

Gas hissed from the cracked pipe!
noise/drama/emotion/order

Question mark

A question mark like this, **?** also comes at the end of a sentence, and is also used in place of a full stop. It indicates that the sentence is a question (as if there wasn't a clue in the name!).

For example:

- ✦ Are we nearly there yet?
- ✦ Your dog ate your homework, did he?
- ✦ What time is the game starting?

Sometimes question marks are used mid-sentence, a bit like a semi-colon to show a series of linked queries:

Now the vase was broken, should he run? own up? hide the pieces?

Technically, these ought to be separate sentences:

Now the vase was broken, should he run? Own up? Hide the pieces?

But you'll find plenty of examples of both versions in books.

Sometimes they can indicate that a piece of information is missing:

Sir Walter Silly (153?-1602) was the nuttiest Tudor in England.

Here the question mark shows that we don't know the exact year of Sir Walter Silly's birth, just that it was fifteen thirty-something-or-other.

Here are some answers. Try making up questions in the space provided (complete with question marks) that could go with them:

Q _____

A It wasn't me, Mrs Jackson. I wasn't even playing football.

Q _____

A John, Felicity, Graham, Ed and Lily.

Q _____

A Twenty-seven.

Q _____

A We went to the shops and Mum bought a new coat.

Q _____

A It's all about the basic rules of grammar.

Q _____

A Yes, officer, I saw a man walking in that direction, wearing a stripy jumper and an eye mask.

Q _____

A Well, it's OK, but not as good as the first film.

Q _____

A Wednesday, definitely.

Q _____

A Spaghetti and salad, please.

Q _____

A Nobody knows for sure, but we know he died in 1602.

Apostrophe

An **apostrophe** like this, ' can be used for two things:

1 To show a possessive - that a noun owns something.

In the sentence, "Callum's bike is blue", the apostrophe shows that the bike belongs to Callum.

The word "Callums" is plural - there's more than one person called Callum. However, "Callum's" with an apostrophe is possessive - it shows that Callum has something.

2 To show that a letter or two is missing.

In the sentences, "I don't like cheese", or, "Class 4 can't spell", the apostrophe means we don't have to say, "I *do not* like cheese", or, "Class 4 *cannot* spell".

Squished up words like *can't, doesn't* or *shouldn't* are called **contractions**.

Add apostrophes in the correct places to the following sentences. If you find it easier, use the space provided to rewrite the sentences with all of the correct apostrophes in place.

1. You dont think Natalies school bag was stolen, do you?

_____

2. The teachers shoes squeaked and he couldnt stop them disturbing the class.

_____

3. Wouldnt the dogs bed be better on the floor than on the ceiling?

_____

4. Cant you see hes unhappy about it?

5. My six cats wont be any bother while Im away.

_____

6. Gemmas about to find out that she shouldnt have cancelled Mums online order.

_____

7. Youre sure this sandwich isnt Georges, but hes sure it is.

_____

8. If Callums got a blue bike, Rosies bike must be the green one.

_____

9. Henrys pet cobra doesnt do tricks.

_____

10. Her friends room was messy, but hers wasnt.

_____

Brackets

You use pairs of **brackets** like this, **( )** when you want to separate a piece of text from a sentence. The bit you're putting in brackets is relevant to the sentence, but not strictly necessary.

For example:

✦ "Sally was keen on boxing (but not other sports) and had won several medals."

"The school cat caught mice (and fleas) behind the bike shelter."

"Pete's trainers (gold and purple Super-Soles) had cost a small fortune."

The brackets give us some background information. You could leave the bracketed bit out and the sentence would still make sense.

Often, brackets are useful for information that goes alongside something:

"The South American flub-flub bird (*Flubbius Birdius*) has brightly coloured wings."

The bracketed bit tells us the bird's scientific name.

There are various forms of brackets, such as [square ones] or {curly ones} or <angled ones> but they all perform the same functions. The proper name for brackets is **parentheses** (pronounced *par-ren-this-ees*).

See if you can place brackets into the following sentences. If you find it easier, use the space provided to rewrite the sentences with the correct brackets in place.

1. Our Maths teacher who lived in America for a while always wears a baseball cap.

   _____

2. Buckingham Palace situated in London is made entirely of crushed-up biscuits.

   _____

3. The photograph printed on page 236 shows us on holiday in Bournemouth.

   _____

4. In our garden is a bush a very big one which needs to be clipped back regularly.

   _____

5. The bird the one with brightly coloured wings was a South American flub-flub.

   _____

6 You can't tell from looking at it or smelling it exactly how old it is.

_____

7 My car an electric Mega-Power 542 is very cheap to run.

_____

8 The pirates left their ship along with the treasure in the Captain's cabin to explore the island.

_____

9 Every member of my family including my niece has enormous ears.

_____

10 Whatever the weather sunshine, rain or snow my Uncle Tim goes for a walk at ten o'clock.

_____

Inverted commas

A set of **inverted commas** like this, **" "** , otherwise known as **quotation marks**, or sometimes **speech marks**, can be used in two ways:

1 They can be used for marking text which directly quotes what somebody has written or said.

For example:

"We've got spaghetti for tea," said Mum.

"We're going to be late," said Olivia.

It says in Mike's email that, "All vegetables are disgusting."

2 They can also be used to pick out a word or group of words in a sentence, to give it special attention or imply an alternative meaning.

For example:

Jack had 'forgotten' his homework.

This implies that Jack hadn't really forgotten it at all.

Helen and her 'arty' friends went to the gallery.

This heavily points out a characteristic of these friends.

The boy band's new download was a 'crash and burn' flop.

This underlines that the nature of the flop was particularly severe.

Inverted commas come in two types:

Single: 'Like this'

Double: "Like this"

Beware! Single inverted commas shouldn't be mistaken for apostrophes!

When should you use 'single' and when should you use "double" inverted commas?

If you're being *strictly* accurate, double inverted commas should only be used when you're placing a quote *inside* another quote.

For example:

> 'My best friend says that "orange juice is made by squirrels" but I don't believe him,' said Tim.

Technically single inverted commas mark a quote and doubles mark a quote-within-a-quote. However, double inverted commas are used so often for quoting speech, that either are perfectly fine to use.

> "I want some cake," said Lisa.

Is really no different to writing:

> 'I want some cake,' said Lisa.

But if you look back to the *Jack had 'forgotten' his homework* example on page 83, you'll see that it uses single inverted commas because they're not actually quoting something somebody said.

A good rule of thumb is: if it's **direct speech**, you can use singles or doubles, if it's **something else**, singles are best.

Inverted commas hints and tips

1 When quoting speech, opening inverted commas are normally followed by a capital letter, wherever they occur in the sentence.

Captain Brilliant exclaimed, "It's up to me to save the world!"
Dr Villain sneered, "You are doomed!"

2 As you might guess from the above examples, when a quote comes at the end of a sentence, the full stop (or exclamation mark, or question mark) normally comes *before* the inverted commas.

Aisling said, "That homework was easy."
Steve replied, "Easy? You call that easy?"

3 You need to put a comma before the last inverted commas of a quote, if the sentence carries on.

"That was a delicious sardine and jam sandwich," said Uncle Slightlymad.

4 When you're quoting direct speech, you need to put a comma *before* the opening inverted commas.

Ed said, "I've completed the Science project."
Julie gasped, "The project was for History, not Science."

Rewrite these sentences in the space provided, including inverted commas and other punctuation where needed.

1. Mrs Johnson said I cant believe youve done that Tony

_____

2. When I grow up said Arthur Im going to be an astronaut

_____

3. Even so-called experts make mistakes yes said Professor Brainful goldfish are very dangerous

_____

4. This so-called computer is actually just an empty box he cried

_____

5. Joe said Liam told me I wasnt allowed to pull faces.

_____

6. Why cant Fred come with us asked Kay

_____

7. Mr Parkers class is well behaved said the Head Teacher

_____

8. The headline in the newspaper declared robots from Mars claim invasion is peace mission

_____

9. Tom and Jane say theyre best friends but I dont believe them

_____

10. Oh hes not feeling well is he sneered David hes just trying to avoid the Maths test

_____

Comma

We've left the humble **comma, ,** until last, because using commas can be deceptively tricky! The role of a comma is to **separate** things.

✶ They can simply provide a pause between one section of a sentence and another:

"For an hour after lunch, we played computer games."

"On a school trip, I always eat my packed lunch before we leave."

✴ They can act a bit like brackets, and separate out parts of a sentence:

"James was, to be honest, very bad at tennis", which could also be expressed as, "James was (to be honest) very bad at tennis"

✴ They can act a bit like semicolons and help you list things:

"Mum bought eggs, butter, cheese and a giant reptile."

"I need pens, paper, glue, cardboard, envelopes and an eraser."

Commas used like this are sometimes called **serial commas**.

✴ They can also have this 'listing' function for groups of words:

"I got up, brushed my teeth, ate my breakfast, put on my uniform, and left for school."

"Our teacher marched in, told us to keep quiet, wrote on the whiteboard, and marched out again."

✴ They can act a bit like conjunctions, and join two ideas together:

"I went to school, everything was fine", which could also be expressed as, "I went to school and everything was fine", or, "I went to school but everything was fine"

✦ They can divide things up so they're easier to understand:

Instead of 90000000 we write 90,000,000.

Or instead of, "I come from Paris France", we write, "I come from Paris, France" to show that Paris and France aren't one place just called 'Paris France'.

In an alphabetical list of names, you'd see 'Smith, Peter' instead of 'Smith Peter' (to show that the name is Peter Smith, not actually 'Smith Peter')

In a sentence such as, "I was born on August 9, 2009", the comma makes it clear that the date wasn't August 92009th!

✦ They can sometimes separate adverbs from the rest of a sentence:

"So, why wasn't he at school?"

"Therefore, the Earth circles the Sun."

"We found out all about the Moon, too."

✦ They can separate pairs of adjectives:

"Paul owned a vicious, ugly rabbit."

"I'm a beautiful, tranquil robot."

Above all, commas are important for helping readers *make* sense of text. Treat them with respect! A misplaced comma can **completely** change the meaning of a sentence:

For example:

What does, "I don't want to ask Katie", mean?

As it is, it means that you're talking to someone who isn't Katie, and telling them that you don't want to ask Katie a question.

However, if you add one comma, "I don't want to ask, Katie", the sentence becomes very different. Here, you're talking to Katie, and telling her that you don't want to ask *anyone* this question.

What does, "I'll send emails to Arun's mum Anne and Emily", mean?

As it is, the meaning isn't clear. You need to add one or two commas, to end up with either one of the following:

"I'll send emails to Arun's mum, Anne and Emily" this means that you'll send <u>three</u> emails, one to Arun's mum, one to Anne and one to Emily.

"I'll send emails to Arun's mum, Anne, and Emily" this means that Arun's mum is *called* Anne (because you've separated out the name Anne from the rest of the sentence) and that you'll send two emails, one to Arun's mum (whose name is Anne) and one to Emily.

Put commas into the following sentences. Be careful not to change the overall meaning. If you find it easier, use the space provided to rewrite the sentences with the correct commas in place.

① The large colourful painting of the King was it must be said a very good likeness.

_____

② When the three chickens crossed the road something they did every day they got to the other side.

_____

③ If you phone Ewan Sara and Richard James can phone Dervla Jonah and Josh.

_____

④ If you include Fred the list of class members with fair hair includes four maybe five people.

_____

⑤ There'll be trouble big trouble if Mum sees you've got paint mud and ink on the carpet.

_____

6) The wide lawns the trees the river and the playground are all features of our local park.

7) Ten paces west six north four east and twelve south is where you'll find the treasure buried.

8) I can't believe that you of all people would say that!

9) She sat quietly waiting for her turn to speak until the spotlight suddenly dazzled her.

10) Nothing not even the promise of ice cream every day could persuade me to go on a camping trip.

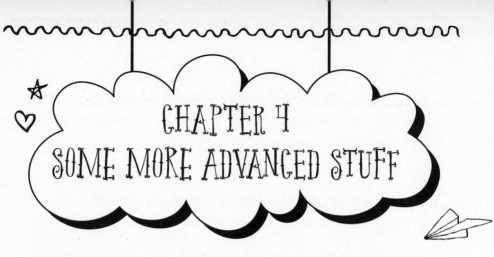

CHAPTER 4
SOME MORE ADVANCED STUFF

So far, we've covered the basic nuts and bolts of punctuation, but there are plenty more we can use to make our sentences shine. Here are just a few.

Dashes

A dash like this, — is used to show a break in something.

For example:

✦ They can create a break in a sentence - just like this - which acts in a similar way to brackets or pairs of commas.

"Joe was - whether he liked it or not - about to start the exam."

Could also be expressed as, "Joe was (whether he liked it or not) about to start the exam."

Or, "Joe was, whether he liked it or not, about to start the exam."

✦ They can create a single break in a sentence too – just like this. It's a way to show that you want to stress, or **emphasise**, what comes after the dash.

"He wrote a series of words in his notebook – in French."

"There are big price cuts on these items – up to 50%."

✦ They can also be a kind of 'shorthand' way to mark a break that means 'from . . . to . . .'

"The stuff about ancient Egypt was on pages 23-36."

"World War II was 1939-1945."

✦ They can also mark a break which means 'this was said by . . .'

"We will fight them on the beaches." – Winston Churchill

"This is the greatest book ever written." – Overthetop Book Reviews

EXAM

Use the space provided to rewrite the sentences by adding a dash or two. You can use them to cut into the sentence, to create emphasis, or to mark a break.

① The monster which was huge, hairy and ugly stomped through the town.

_____

② Nobody else in the class got question three right only you.

_____

③ There were something like 10 20 people waiting in the queue.

_____

④ On several days including Wednesday Josh took the dog for a walk.

_____

⑤ I've never seen anything like it never

_____

SOME MORE ADVANCED STUFF

6. My brothers and sisters were born in the period 2007 2014.

7. Where else apart from a museum could we have seen such an ancient object?

8. You must not under any circumstances open that door.

9. "This is excellent work, James, well done" Mrs Jones, Class 6J.

10. There were hundreds of mice hundreds, I tell you running around the barn.

Hyphens

A **hyphen** like this, **—** is used to either **break up** individual words, or **stick them together**. Yes, call the Confusion Police, a hyphen looks just like a dash! Although they look alike, it's *what they're* used for that makes the difference.

✦ Hyphens can break words into pieces. For example, if you need to talk about parts of a word, as in *the word badly is a -ly adverb.*

✦ They're useful for cutting up words in direct speech when you want to indicate how a word is being said.

The robot shouted "Des-troy! Des-troy!"

"That is ab-sol-ute-ly brilliant work."

✦ Hyphens can join words together to make new ones.

"I told a spine-tingling story to my ten-year-old son about how I fought a man-eating shark."

"Watering down ketchup is a cost-effective way to make it last from mid-October to Christmas.

Other examples are, X-ray, finely-tuned or self-assured.

✦ Two-digit numbers, when written out in words, are normally hyphenated:

Twenty-seven, ninety-one, one hundred and sixty-four.

✦ Sometimes, hyphens are used to join names:

"Hi, my name is Wayne Smith-Parsley."

"I found the definition in the Merbster-Oxbridge Dictionary of Strange Words."

ACTIVITY

Place hyphens into the correct place(s) in these phrases. If you find it easier, use the space provided to rewrite the phrases with hyphens in the correct place.

The highest scoring team

_____

Ninety six thousand ants

_____

Godfrey Thompson Harris, MP

_____

A nerve wracking English exam

_____
_____

"That's utterly impossible!"

_____

The mid Winter festival

A semi retired teacher

A pack of pre sliced cheese

A sense of self importance

Many five door vehicles

Ellipses

An ellipsis like this, **. . .** is used to indicate a **pause**, a **missing bit**, or a **gap** . . .

- The ellipsis on the line above shows that instead of saying *for example*, you can miss that bit out because it's obvious what comes next.
- Ellipses can indicate many sorts of missing bits such as gaps in sequences.

  If you write, 1, 2, 3, 4 . . . 19, 20, you're indicating that the sequence continues after 4 and carries on until we get to 20. You don't need to write out every number in the sequence.
- Ellipses are useful in speech to indicate a pause:

"It's not that I don't believe you but... are you saying your Maths teacher is a Martian?"

- You can use an ellipsis to indicate that an idea remains unfinished, or to imply something that remains unsaid:

  "To this day, the fate of that damaged sailing ship is a mystery . . ."

Colons

A **colon** like this, **:** is used at the start of lists, or to *introduce* some sort of logical follow-on. At the end of this sentence, it's showing that a list follows:

For example:

✭ Almost any **list** or **sequence** can follow a colon.

"Here are my reasons for not eating vegetables:"

✭ A colon can introduce a **logical conclusion.**

"Jack never listened in class: his exams were a disaster."

✭ A colon can introduce a **description** or **explanation.**

"Our Science teacher is sorry: he looks like a monster."

✭ You can use colons to introduce an order or **command.**

"Don't forget: wash your hands."

✭ Colons are often used in the titles of movies or games.

Cuddly Teddies II: The Revenge

Here, the colon divides a title from its 'sub-title' (meaning a secondary title or sub-heading).

Semicolons

A **semicolon** like this, **;** is used to **connect** linked sentences. While a colon shows a firm logical link between two ideas, a semicolon just shows that two things go together.

For example:

✠ "The football smashed the window: the player received a large bill."

This sentence needs a colon, as the bill is a logical consequence of the smash.

"The football smashed the window; several got smashed that day."

This sentence only needs a semicolon as the two statements are linked, but one doesn't strictly follow on from the other.

✠ Semicolons often follow colons in a list.

"The teacher set out his policies: loads of homework; tests every Friday; snakes in the playground."

You don't have to use semicolons for a 'colon' list (you could have *my best friends: Rob, Violet, Tim . . .*) but semicolons are more usual.

Slashes

A **slash** like this, **/** is a symbol which can be used as a replacement for the words 'or' or 'also'.

"I'm an actor/ singer/ model."

"We're expecting the results of the experiment during April/ May/ June."

Did you know?

The term 'slash' (or 'forward slash') was only created because computer programmers didn't know what the correct word for this symbol was. It's actually called a **stroke** or a **solidus**. That's also why a full stop gets incorrectly called a 'dot' in web addresses!

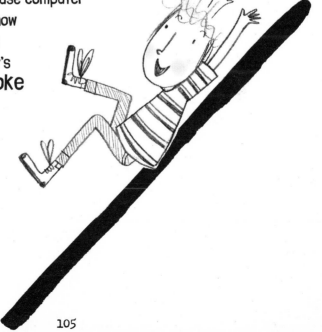

105

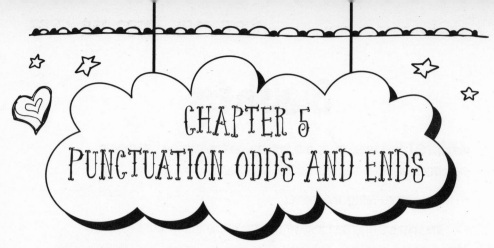

CHAPTER 5
PUNCTUATION ODDS AND ENDS

Here are some bits and pieces which, strictly speaking, aren't actually punctuation but they are things you often see, and which you can use in everyday written communication. To be accurate, these items are *typographical* (typography is to do with how text is printed).

Asterisks

An asterisk like this, * is used for two main reasons:

1 To flag or make a note of something in text.

It alerts you to the presence of a footnote, which is a note that accompanies the text, usually at the bottom of the page.*

2 Asterisks can also be used to indicate missing information, a bit like ellipses. However, it's information which you deliberately want to leave out:

*"My teacher is ** years old."*

*Like this one here.

106

Bullets

A **bullet** like this, • is a symbol used to itemise things in a list, like this:

- Here's the first item

- And here's the second, which is followed by

- Number three!

Look back through this book, and you'll see loads of them! Some books will change the shape of the bullets - in this book, stars often take the place of bullets!

Ampersand

An **ampersand** like this, **&** is a symbol which can stand in for the word 'and'.

Grabbit & Snatchem Ltd., Accountants

Shopping Centre Fish & Chips

Simple as that!

107

'At'

A symbol like this, **@**, referred to as 'at', is used in email addresses:

Ilovegrammar@grammar.com

Thisbookisawesome@ilovebooks.com

This is properly called a 'commercial at' and was originally used in Italy and Spain during Tudor times to denote a unit of weight!

Hashtag

A symbol like this, **#** is generally known as a 'hashtag'. In fact it has several names, including 'hatch', 'number sign', 'pound' and 'octothorpe.' Until computers were invented, it was mainly used to indicate a number in a series:

This is book #2 of the author's detective stories.

Copyright symbols

You'll see symbols such as © or ® or ™ printed in lots of books or on products. These are special legal symbols, which mark ownership of things such as fictional characters, movies or designs.

Spend some time looking carefully through

1 A newspaper

2 A fiction book

3 A non-fiction book

Notice the ways in which they use punctuation. What differences can you spot? How do they use punctuation to organise words? Can you think of alternative ways to punctuate some of their sentences? Use the space provided to have a go at rewriting some of the sentences you come across.

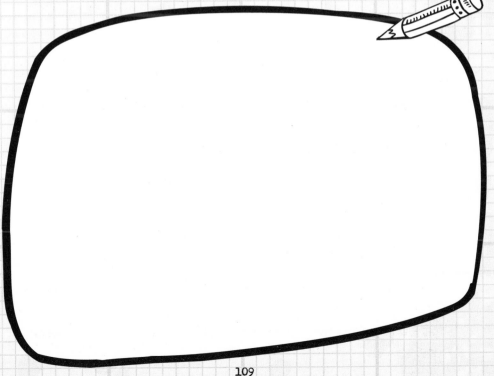

They begin with a capital letter. They end with a full stop (or another terminal). If words are the building blocks of language, then **sentences** are its walls and ceilings, the basic **structure** of communication. How are they assembled? What are they for?

Before we can understand how sentences are constructed, we need to know about . . .

Phrases

A **phrase** is any short 'unit' of words which expresses a single idea or thought:

The smelly sock, a sunny afternoon, he's late, going for a walk, her blue bicycle, against the odds, under the table – these are all phrases.

A phrase is the smallest bit of a sentence that still makes sense without the rest of the sentence. *The smelly sock* makes sense, we understand the **meaning** of the phrase, but **on its own** it's not a complete sentence - it's a phrase.

There are lots of different **types** of phrases: noun phrases, verb phrases, gerund phrases, prepositional phrases, and plenty of others. Don't worry, we're not going to investigate them all - we'd fill up the rest of this book and spill over onto the back cover as well!

Clauses

It's nothing to do with Santa! A **clause** is a slightly bigger 'unit' of words, one which has a noun and a verb, plus whatever other bits and pieces it needs in order to express a complete idea.

Dad washed the smelly sock, the cat sat on the mat, my sister likes dancing the tango, we caught the bus into town – these are all clauses.

There are lots of different **types** of clause, too: predicative, adjunct, relative... oh, there are loads! However, most of the time there are only two types you need know about.

1 A **main** or **independent** clause is one which could be a sentence all on its own.

"The rabbit ate the carrot."

"The goat made a smell."

2 A **dependent** or **subordinate** clause is one which wouldn't make sense as a sentence on its own.

"Because carrots taste nice."

"After we'd finished our lunch."

What's the difference between a phrase and a clause?

It's sometimes hard to tell one from the other. Top linguists – people who study languages – have argued over this point for years! An easy rule of thumb is that phrases are normally short and simple, while clauses are normally longer and more complicated.

Which leads us on to:

Sentences

The simplest full **sentence** is made up of a single clause – otherwise called an **independent clause**.

"The team won the cricket match."

"This bin is full of rubbish."

Just stick a capital letter at the start, and a full stop at the end, and it's a sentence! Ta-dah! This sort of sentence is called (no surprises here!) a **simple sentence**.

Sentences often have three components:

1 The **subject** of the sentence:

Who or what 'performs the action' of the sentence. The subject is normally a noun or pronoun.

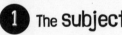

"<u>Dave</u> ran to the shop."

"<u>The monster</u> scared the scientist."

The subject isn't necessarily the first noun in the sentence. For example:

"The peas were squashed by my fork."

In this sentence it's *my fork* that's the subject, because it's the fork that does the action – the squashing.

2 A **verb** (sometimes called the sentence's 'predicate'):

This is the 'action' bit of a sentence.

"Dave *ran* to the shop."

"The monster *scared* the scientist."

3 The **object** of the sentence:

Who or what is 'influenced' by the verb, or 'receives' the action of the verb. Objects are also normally nouns or pronouns.

"Dave ran to *the shop*."

"The monster scared *the scientist*."

The most basic structure of a simple sentence is **subject-verb-object:**

"Fred (subject) dropped (verb) the book (object)."

"Mum (subject) drove (verb) the truck (object)."

Below is a blank table. Fill in the boxes to include a subject, verb and object to make some simple sentences.

SUBJECT	VERB	OBJECT

Now try the same thing but the other way around. Create some simple sentences, which begin with the object instead of the subject.

OBJECT	VERB	SUBJECT

However, this **subject-verb-object** idea isn't a hard-and-fast rule. Sentences can sometimes contain only a subject and a verb/predicate.

For example:

"The bird took flight."
"The babies wailed."

Also, sentences can have . . .

✦ More than one subject:

"<u>Ben and Arthur</u> rode their bikes."

"<u>The girl and her pet mouse</u> passed their exams."

✦ More than one object:

"Ben rode <u>his bike and his scooter.</u>"

"The mouse bought <u>cheese and pickle.</u>"

Sometimes, particularly in speech, you find sentences, often exclamations or interjections, composed of a single word.

For example:

No! Think! Where? Help! Jack!

These are simply called **word sentences**, and a word that makes one is called a **sentence word**.

As sentences get more complicated, they gain words and clauses. The more complicated a sentence is, the more information and detail it contains.

Clauses can be . . .

✳ Joined by conjunctions.

"We stayed after school *and* finished our art project."

"The police chased the thief *but* he got away."

✳ 'Nested' between or inside other clauses.

"We finished the lesson, filled with the joy of grammar, and went out into the playground."

"He hoped, being such a black-hearted villain, to get away with it."

Sentences which have two or more clauses are called **compound** or **complex** sentences.

Here are some **simple** sentences. Add extra clauses to make them into **compound** sentences which tell us more about their subjects (or objects!).

For example:

One clause: Hubert fed the leopard.

Three clauses: Hubert fed the leopard but, because he didn't notice the polished floor, slipped over and got eaten himself.

(1) **The boulder rolled down the hill.**

_____

(2) **Francesca painted a portrait.**

_____

(3) **The aeroplane flew to New York.**

_____

(4) **My aunt came to visit us.**

_____

5 Kevin caught the bus.

_____

6 I don't like broccoli.

_____

7 Dad loves watching soap operas.

_____

8 I mowed the lawn.

_____

9 The alligator swam downstream.

_____

10 The fire fighter put on her boots.

_____

Now we've seen *how* sentences are built, let's look at what we can we *do* with them.

Sentences can serve several different functions.

For example:

✗ A sentence is usually a **statement** - it says something factual:

"Tom went swimming on Tuesday."

"I really can't understand this recipe."

"Victor was the star player in the school ice hockey team."

Most of the sentences we use are statement or 'declarative' sentences. It doesn't matter whether *what* it's declaring is true or false, fiction or non-fiction, it's the fact that the sentence sets out a particular idea, opinion or message that makes it a **statement** sentence.

✦ We normally put **questions** in the form of a sentence:

"Where are you going?"

"What sort of time do you call this, young man?"

"Do I have to give Granny a kiss?"

Questions are 'interrogative' sentences, meaning they 'inquire' about something, or need a reply.

✦ Sentences can also be **orders**:

"Get down from there!"

"Wake up and drink your tea!"

"Leave this school and never return!"

✦ Or **exclamations**:

"You've got to be joking!"

"Look out below!"

"I can't believe you said that!"

Major and minor sentences

If you ask someone, "What time will we be leaving today?" And they answer, "We'll be leaving at four o'clock", they are using a **major** sentence.

If they answer, "Four", they are using a **minor** sentence.

Both answers make sense and are easy to understand, but they are using different types of sentences to convey the same information.

✴ A **major** sentence is any regular sentence. A sentence that contains nouns, verbs, a clause or two, and whatever else we'd expect to find in a properly structured sentence.

✴ A **minor** sentence is an irregular sentence. It is a sentence that often leaves out a verb in order to be brief, or to emphasise a noun. Minor sentences don't usually contain a complete clause.

Wow!   Awesome!   Hi!

These exclamations are minor sentences when used on their own (and also 'word sentences').

Minor sentences can be phrases such as:

"The more the merrier."
"Better safe than sorry."
"Like father like son."

Some headings or headlines can be minor sentences, such as, *TV Star In Cake Shock*.

You find quite a lot of minor sentences in poetry, and catchphrases are often minor sentences.

ACTIVITY

Pick a couple of pages at random in a fiction book. Try to categorise the individual sentences according to their function and type – statement sentences, minor sentences, orders, major sentences and so on.

Active and passive voice

Just like verbs, sentences can also have an **active** or **passive** voice. It all depends on who or what in the sentence is carrying out the action described.

✦ **Active:** "Zoe chased the elephant, I cooked the spaghetti."

✦ **Passive:** "The elephant was chased by Zoe, the spaghetti was cooked by me."

Quick rule of thumb: if the verb is followed with the word 'by' it's normally a passive sentence.

Subject-verb agreement

In any sentence, you need to think of the verb and the subject of the sentence as best friends. They need to agree with each other:

✦ If the subject is singular (one on its own) then the verb should be singular too:

"The teddy bear (singular) is (singular) brown."

✦ If the subject is plural (more than one) then the verb should be plural:

"The teddy bears (plural) are (plural) brown."

Take note! Be careful about identifying the sentence's subject . . .

For example:

✦ "That film (singular) about dinosaurs (plural) <u>was</u> (singular) brilliant."

OR

"That film (singular) about dinosaurs (plural) <u>were</u> (plural) brilliant."

Which is correct?

You need *was*, not *were*, because it's the film that's the subject of the sentence, not the dinosaurs. If you said, "Those films (plural) about dinosaurs (plural) were (plural) brilliant" then you'd need *were*, because you've now got more than one film.

⭐ Be careful when the subject comes after the verb in a sentence:

"On my wall are lots of posters."

There's only one wall, but it's *posters* that's the subject of the sentence. You need to use *are* (plural) to agree with *posters* (plural).

"On my wall is lots of posters", would not be correct.

⭐ Be careful when you have more than one subject in a sentence:

"Dan and Jane are very tall."

Here, both people are the sentence's subject, so you need *are*. You'd need *is* if you said, "Dan is very tall and Jane is very tall", but put them together as one subject and you need that plural.

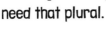

Make sure these sentences have verbs and subjects which agree with each other by filling in the blanks with appropriate verbs (in some cases, you may find that different verbs can fit the same spaces).

1. Nick, Fiona and Gus _____ the brainiest pupils in Class B.

2. This tin of beans _____ incorrectly priced, but these tins _____ priced correctly.

3. The flood _____ up to my knees!

4. These sheep _____ plenty of grass.

5. A fleet of aircraft _____ at the airport.

6) Four bags of carrots _____ in the shopping trolley, but one bag _____ split.

7) Our school _____ many teachers – in fact, most schools _____ many teachers.

8) My book about Kings and Queens _____ very interesting.

9) This sentence _____ short, but those sentences _____ long.

10) Taking part in the dance contest _____ Harry and Fiona.

Now you know about words, punctuation and sentences, you're well on your way to understanding the basics of grammar. However, grammar also has some unusual quirks and interesting aspects . . .

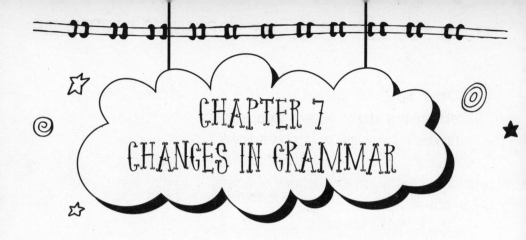

CHAPTER 7
CHANGES IN GRAMMAR

There's *always* debate about whether something is bad grammar, or simply a natural change in the English language.

Grammar can change over time

It used to be correct grammar to place the 'an' participle in front of every word beginning with the letter 'h':

An horse, an horrific nightmare, an hotel, an history book . . .

These days, it's fine to say *a horse, a horrific nightmare.*

Although, there are exceptions – we still say *an hour* or *an honour.*

Punctuation changes a lot. It used to be quite common to see exclamation marks in the middle of sentences:

"The hero jumped! but missed the train."

Today, that 'but' would need a capital letter.

Grammar can change from place to place

A 'dialect' is a way of using language that's shared by people within certain groups or locations. English dialects used in different parts of the world can vary in their grammar. For example, in the southern states of America you get 'doubled-up' negatives:

"Nobody here ain't never been to New York", instead of just, "Nobody here has been to New York."

Some Scottish dialects use prepositions differently:

"She took the ketchup *off of* the table" (instead of just 'off the table').

"We were waiting *on* you" (instead of 'waiting for you').

Listen carefully to people in the UK who speak in different regional accents, and you'll notice grammatical variations. You often find, for example, non-standard uses of the verb 'to be'.

Instead of *'I was'* and *'they were'* you find forms such as, *'I were'* and *'they was'*:

"I were just leaving school when I saw the alien spaceship."

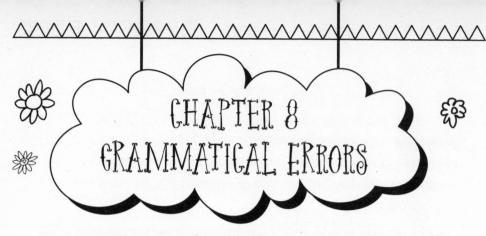

CHAPTER 8
GRAMMATICAL ERRORS

Grammar can be complicated, so it's easy for mistakes to crop up. Here are some common errors to watch out for, and avoid. There are lots and lots of others, many of which drive some nit-picking adults totally bonkers!

This / That / Who

Objects are 'this' and 'that', but people are 'who'. It's incorrect to say: "The person that wrote this book." It should be: "The person who wrote this book." "The pen that was used to write this book", would be correct, because a pen is an object.

Its and it's

You should only use it's when you're missing out letters. For example, *it is, it has, it was*. Its (without the apostrophe) means something that belongs to it. So, "It's past three o'clock" is correct (it is past three o'clock). But "The dragon folded it's wings", is incorrect, it should be "the dragon folded *its* wings."

Apostrophes

They show possession not plurals. Simply adding 's' to a noun only makes it plural. You need 'apostrophe-s' if you mean that the noun *owns* something (yes, *it's* and *its* are an exception!)

Correct: "This is my mum's car." "These carrots are 90p."
Incorrect: "This is my mums car." "These carrot's are 90p."

Me, myself and I

How should you refer to yourself in sentences? People often make two mistakes:

1 Using 'I' instead of 'me'

For example: "Jill made tea for Peter and I" (it should be, 'Peter and *me*'). However, it's correct to say, "Peter and I made tea for Jill" (not 'Peter and *me*'). The way to work out what's correct here is to eliminate Peter (poor guy!). Take him out of the sentences and it's obvious that, "Jill made tea for I" and, "Me made tea for Jill", sound silly!

2 Using 'myself' instead of 'me'

You often hear people say things like, "The project was run by John and myself" or "P.C. Jones and myself chased the thief". Again, the solution is to cut out other people from the sentence and the answer becomes clear: "The project was run by . . . me", and, "I . . . chased the thief".

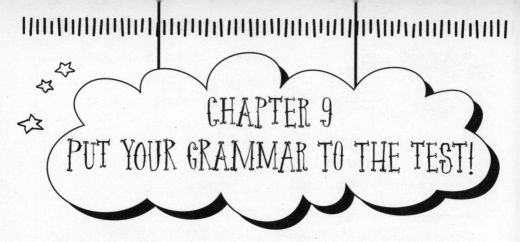

CHAPTER 9
PUT YOUR GRAMMAR TO THE TEST!

Grammar can be a tricky subject but by knowing the basic rules, you can polish up your writing in no time!

Above all, there is no substitute for *reading*. The more you read, the better you'll be at identifying correct (and incorrect!) grammar when you see it.

Keep in mind all the advice and information you've encountered in this book, and you'll be able to construct your sentences with confidence!

Put what you've learned to the test and try the following activities!

|||||||||||||||||||||||||||| PUT YOUR GRAMMAR TO THE TEST

It's the seven-sentence challenge! Test the knowledge you've gained from this book by using the space provided to complete seven sentences, which together form a mini-story. Make sure your grammar is **100%** accurate!

At random, pick characters from the first column, then pick a situation or activity from the second column, and finally add a grammatical feature to use somewhere in your seven-sentence story from the third column.

When you've finished . . . pick some more and have another go! Your sentences can be as wacky as you like, just as long as the grammar is correct!

CHARACTERS	SITUATION	GRAMMATICAL FEATURE
Two school friends	Choosing a book to read	Lots of direct speech
A police officer and a bank robber	Taking a train journey	Colons and semi-colons
Your head teacher and one of the dinner ladies	Doing some gardening	Possessives (using apostrophes)
A superhero and the Prime Minister	Shopping in the supermarket	Loads of adjectives and adverbs
Two hedgehogs	Writing an essay	As many interjections as possible (not onomatopoeias!)
A knight in armour and a dragon	Looking for something they've lost	Major and minor sentences
Two people who speak different languages	Watching a TV show	Three (or more!) clauses in one sentence
A cat and a dog	Cooking their dinner	Brackets or dashes

Two aliens	Taking a day off at the beach	Plenty of prepositions and conjunctions
A singer and a painter	Visiting as museum	More than one subject in a sentence
A secret agent and his/her granny	Creeping through a spooky old house	Using active and passive voices for verbs
A doctor and a patient	Mending something that's been broken	Using inverted commas, but not for direct speech
Someone very tall and someone very short	Racing each other to get somewhere first	Include the same word more than once, but used as different parts of speech
You and your worst enemy	Playing a sport	Use commas in their 'listing' function
Two people who speak different languages	Watching a TV show	Three (or more!) clauses in one sentence
A cat and a dog	Cooking their dinner	Brackets or dashes

Use the space provided to rewrite the following sentences so that there are no grammatical errors. (Beware - some things might already be correct!).

1. When Rachel and me returned, all the crisp's had gone and there were less peanuts in the bowl!

_____

_____

2. Its up to you who sets out the tables, but the person that does must put the tablecloths out, too.

_____

_____

3. No fewer than twelve medals were won at this years chess tournament, the highest total in it's history.

_____

_____

4. Thanks to mine Mums quick thinking, that games kit of mine didn't get forgot today.

_____

_____

5. Mary have extra lessons in Science, but less than David, Gina or I.

_____

_____

6 The dragon has breathing fire from it's mouth as it flown over the mountain.

_____

_____

7 A spaceship who was contained astronauts lands on the surface of the Moon.

_____

_____

8 If it's a book about grammar you're want, my teachers got loads of it.

_____

_____

9 I sing beautifully, I draw beautifully and I written also beautifully, its true.

_____

_____

10 Mrs Jones pet tarantula run through the Year 6 classroom and frightened the children that was doing his History project.

_____

_____

MORE WRITING SPACE